A is for Addax

The ABC's of Endangered and Threatened Animals

Written and Illustrated by Suzanne Fear

ISBN: 0692864784
ISBN-13: 978-0692864784

DEDICATION

For my family and my friends, who have supported me in all of my endeavors.

Our world is full of creatures, big and small. All of the animals in this book are endangered or threatened, which means if we don't protect them some day there won't be any of them at all.

A is for Addax

B is for Bobcat

C is for Cheetah

D is for Dhole

E is for Elephant

F is for Fossa

G is for Gibbon

H is for Hyena

I is for Ibex

J is for Jaguar

K is for Kakapo

L is for Lynx

M is for Manatee

N is for Numbat

O is for Orangutan

P is for Pangolin

Q is for Quokka

R is for Rhinoceros [23]

S is for Saola

T is for Tapir

U is for Uakari

V is for Vaquita

W is for Wolf

X is for aXolotl

Y is for Yak

Z is for Zebra

Addax – (ad-aks) Addax are large antelope that live in the Sahara desert. They have long flat hooves to help them to keep balance on the shifting sand dunes that make up their homes.

Bobcat – (bob-kat) Bobcats are medium sized wildcats with short stubby tails that live throughout North America. Bobcats prefer to live by themselves in large spacious territories.

Cheetah – (chee-tuh) Cheetahs are large wild cats that live in Eastern and Southern Africa. They are the fastest animal on land. They use their long tails to help them keep their balance while they run.

Dhole – (dohl) Dhole are a type of wild dog that live throughout Central, South and Southeast Asia. They are very social animals that live together in groups called packs, and use their keen senses of smell to find prey.

Elephant – (el-uh-fuh nt) Elephants are the largest land mammals. They live in both Africa and Asia. Elephants live together in families that are led by the oldest female elephant in the group. African Elephants use their large ears to fan themselves to keep cool in hot temperatures.

Fossa – (fos-uh) Fossa are cat like mammals that live in Madagascar. They have very good night vision and are excellent hunters. They use their retractable claws to easily climb trees.

Gibbon – (gib-uh n) Gibbon are small apes that live throughout South East Asia. They are very social creatures that pair off and mate for life. They use their long arms to help them swing from tree to tree.

Hyena – (hahy-ee-nuh) Hyenas are large carnivorous animals that resemble dogs that live throughout Africa. They live in groups called clans, and hunt together as a unit. Their barks are often compared to a human's cackle or laugh.

Ibex – (ahy-beks) Ibex are a species of wild goats that live in the Alpine mountains of Europe. They live in groups in very steep environments. The male Ibex use their long curved horns to fight for the attention of the female Ibex.

Jaguar – (jag-wahr) Jaguar are a type of large panther that live in South America as well as the southernmost part of North America. Jaguars prefer to live in swampy areas, and love swimming. The large spots that cover a Jaguar's body help it to blend in and hide in its environment.

Kakapo – (kah-kuh-poh) Kakapo are large flightless birds that live on the island of New Zeeland. Kakapo live underground in burrows and are nocturnal, which means they are mostly active at night.

Lynx – (lingks) Lynx are a type of medium-sized wildcat that live in Central Asia, Canada, and Southern Europe. Lynx have short bobbed tails, and dark tufts of fur that stick out from the tips of their ears. They are solitary animals and are very shy. Their thick fur coats help to keep them warm in the cold environments they live in.

Manatee – (man-uh-tee) Manatee are large aquatic mammals that live in the warm waters of west India, South America, and West Africa. They eat mostly plants, and use there flat teeth to grind them. Manatee are also very intelligent and have good long-term memories.

Numbat – (nuhm-bat) Numbat are small marsupials that live in Western Australia. Numbats eat primarily termites. They use their long claws to dig them up, and then use their long sticky tongues to catch as many as possible.

Orangutan – (aw-rang-oo-tan) Orangutan are a type of great ape that live in the rainforests of Indonesia and Malaysia. They spend most of their time in the treetops. Orangutans are very intelligent animals and use many tools. They sleep in carefully built nests high up in the trees they call home.

Pangolin – (pang-guh-lin) Pangolin live throughout Africa and parts of Asia. Pagolin are covered in hard interlocking scales that help protect them from predators. They use there long sharp claws to dig up termite mounds; termites are a Pangolins favorite food. When Pangolin are frightened they curl up into a tiny ball to hide.

Quokka – (kwok-uh) Quokka are a type of short tailed marsupial that live on small islands of the coast of Western Australia. They live in small groups and are mostly active at night. Female Quokkas have pouches that they use to carry their young around much like a Kangaroo.

Rhinoceros – (rahy-nos-er-uh s) Rhinoceros are large land mammals that live in Africa and Southeast Asia. Rhinoceros have tough thick skin and strong muscular bodies to make them difficult for predators to hunt. They use the long horns on their noses to fend off predators and dig up food.

Saola – (saw-oh-la) Saola are a type of forest dwelling herbivore that are closely related to cows. They live in the Annamite Mountains of Vietnam and Laos. They are very shy and quite animals that were only officially discovered in 1992.

Tapir – (tey-per) Tapir are large herbivores that live in the jungles and forests of South America. Tapirs love the water, and spend most of their time cooling off in it. Tapirs also like to eat the plants and mosses that grow on the bottom of riverbeds. They use their trunk like noses to sniff out food.

Uakari – (wah-kahr-ee) Uakari are a type of bald headed monkey that live in South America. They live in groups and use their powerful arms and legs to swing and leap from branch to branch. Uakari primarily eat fruits, nuts, and other vegetation.

Vaquita – (va-key-ta) Vaquita are a very rare type of porpoise that live in the northern area of the Gulf of California. Vaquita are very shy and tend to avoid boats and coming to the surface of the water as much as possible.

Wolf – (woo lf) Wolves are large pack animals that live on every continent except Australia. Wolves live in family groups called packs. Wolves howl to communicate with other wolves both with and outside of their pack.

Axolotl – (ak-suh-lot-l) Axolotl are a type of salamander that live in Mexico. Axolotls in the wild are normally greyish green. The frills on the sides of an axolotl's face help it to breath in the water.

Yak – (yak) Yaks are a type of wild cow that live in the Himalayas in Central Asia. Female Yaks live in large herds with their young, while male Yaks roam around in solitary or in small groups. Yaks are covered in thick course fur to keep them warm in their very cold environment.

Zebra – (zee-bruh) The Mountain Zebra is a type of Zebra that lives in the dry rocky mountains of South Africa. Mountain Zebra live in small herds and travel together to keep safe from predators. The stripes on their bodies make them seem larger to predators.

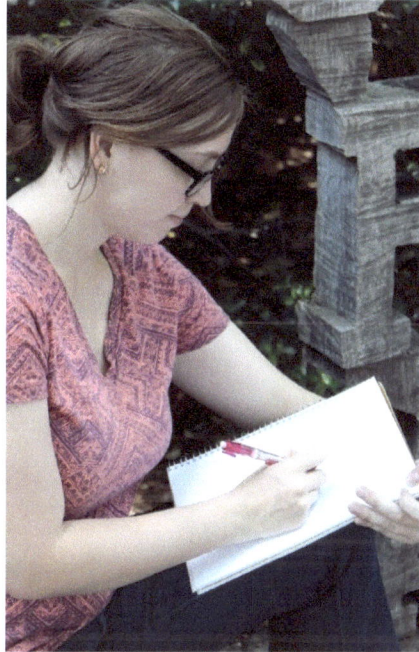

ABOUT THE AUTHOR

Suzanne Fear is an aspiring author and illustrator. This is her first book. She loves animals, sewing, and all things art related. She lives in the north Texas area with her dog Roxie. She can be reached at suzannecfear@gmail.com You can see more of her work at suzannefearillustrations.wordpress.com